Happy B'day from C.H.

LIFE
SOWETO
STYLE

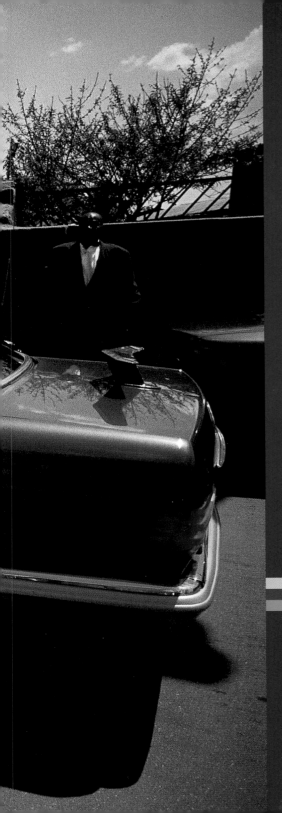

MARK LANNING   NEIL ROAKE   GLYNIS HORNING

LIFE – SOWETO STYLE

Struik Publishers
(a division of New Holland Publishing
   (South Africa) (Pty) Ltd)
Cornelis Struik House
80 McKenzie Street
Cape Town 8001

New Holland Publishing is a member of
   the Johnnic Publishing Group

First published in 2003
10 9 8 7 6 5 4 3 2 1

Publishing manager: Linda de Villiers
Editor: Joy Clack
Designer: Petal Palmer
Cover designer: Kim de Beer
Design assistant: Sean Robertson
Photographer: Mark Lanning
Photographer's assistant: Phinias Ndlovu
Printing of black and white
   photographs: Renelle Rampersad

Reproduction by Hirt & Carter Cape (Pty) Ltd
Printed and bound by Craft (Pte) Ltd, Singapore

ISBN 1 86872 844 7

www.struik.co.za

Log on to our photographic website
www.imagesofafrica.co.za
for an African experience

ACKNOWLEDGEMENTS
Our thanks to the people of Soweto for their help
and hospitality, especially Stanley Kgosana,
Kagiso Malefane, Neo Mashigo, Vusi Mashinini,
Hlalele Wesley Molefi, James Moleko and
Thami Tikolo. We're especially indebted to tour
operator Joe Motsogi (083 3076038), who first
took us into Soweto. Warm thanks too to Pete
(The Funky Monkey) for allowing us to use some
of the fabulous traditional South African recipes he
collects, and to Paul Zeidler for help in researching
South African ingredients.

CONTENTS

hip, hop and happening

Democratic South Africa was born on these streets, and they burn still with an **irresistible energy**, an overwhelming **exuberance of spirit.** It judders defiantly from minibus disco taxis pumping Jozi FM kwaito at killer volumes, and soars majestically from the saxes of old-timers slouched on shady corners. Soweto's street culture is a celebration of this spirit, of inspiration and creativity in the teeth of adversity, and style is everywhere – in its pyramids of plastic-perfect fruits in basins on the pavements, its sharp young dressers, its hand-painted street signs, its shipping container shops and mobile dry-cleaning depots, and its struggle monuments now spearing the vast blue sky.

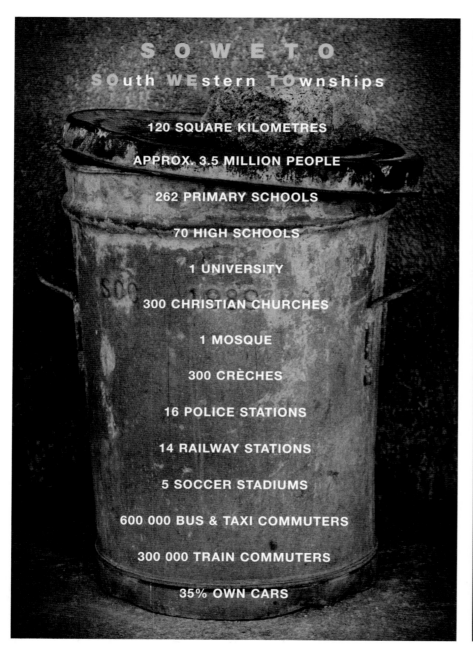

S O W E T O
SOuth WEstern TOwnships

120 SQUARE KILOMETRES

APPROX. 3.5 MILLION PEOPLE

262 PRIMARY SCHOOLS

70 HIGH SCHOOLS

1 UNIVERSITY

300 CHRISTIAN CHURCHES

1 MOSQUE

300 CRÈCHES

16 POLICE STATIONS

14 RAILWAY STATIONS

5 SOCCER STADIUMS

600 000 BUS & TAXI COMMUTERS

300 000 TRAIN COMMUTERS

35% OWN CARS

'I dig you most, my brother'

Soweto was finally electrified in 1985, bringing light to millions,
though informal settlements remain unplugged.

Cold water power to the people.

Sky-blue public phone containers, multicoloured murals, economy sacks of *kip kips* (cheese puffs) billowing from street stalls like fat orange clouds above ruddy pyramids of tomatoes. First shock of Soweto is its colours, rioting against the blandness of identical small houses that march across these extraordinary 120 square kilometres south-west of Johannesburg. Then its shapes seduce your eye, from the writhing 'sculptures' of second-hand exhaust pipes and side mirrors offered on the pavements, to the shimmering squares of custom-cut iron sold for instant *mkhukhus* (shacks).

Sowetans, it's obvious, are an exceptionally enterprising people. And that's what forms their multi-ethnic culture and shapes their street-smart style. Take Bumper Man on one sunny corner of Orlando, with his baggy jeans, full-on attitude and a half-rusted trampoline. Here kids can catapult into the smoky afternoon air for 'Just 30 cents, my brothers!' – flipping and falling in 15 minutes of elastic ecstasy, the limits of life fabulously forgotten until he waves them from his 'bumper' with a switch of plastic hose. 'Next!'

Trainee DJs from Soweto's Jozi FM spin vinyl in their Dube studios.

Entrepreneurial roots sprout early in Soweto, and outside the homes of its most venerated elders, Nelson Mandela and fellow Nobel Peace Prize winner Archbishop Desmond Tutu, children no older than eight serenade you with *Nkosi Sikelel' iAfrika* for a couple of coins, or dance to cowhide drums – a swirling blur of traditional beads and goatskin skirts and Lycra cycle shorts.

But enterprise in Soweto is best exemplified by its shebeen queens, those celebrated tavern keepers who turn their modest homes into the hearts and stomachs of their communities. Today, shebeens range from the unabashedly up-market Wandie's Place in Dube, with its gleaming brass name plaque and 40-dish buffet, where eager tourists call Wandie's cell to wheedle bookings, to the diner-style Flava Resturant [*sic*] in Rockville, a favourite traffic cop haunt, where T-bone with beetroot, pap and beer costs less than R20 (US$2 or 2 Euros at time of going to print).

But the soul of Soweto lies in simple, neighbourhood shebeens like Hilary's Tavern in Dube. Hostess Ruth Maswabi waves you warmly past a well-hung wash line and carefully shone Beetle in her small backyard to a crowded kitchen. Here, old women stir spicy mutton stew in vast pots on a coal stove, and ladle it over pale piles of *pap* (stiff porridge). Ruth pours sweet, chilled *mqombothi* (traditional sorghum beer) from a calabash, and invites you to savour it in the family lounge – a fabulously florid affair of heavily carved furniture, lino-lined walls, and floral drapes drifting from pelmets where carved guineafowl jostle with ornamental beer mugs.

Serious local drinkers are diverted to a simpler outside room, where hard music and harder drinks rule. 'My customers are my family,' says Ruth when she sees you out, steering you firmly past raucous laughter and a thumping hip-hop beat, 'But they do less damage out there. You must use good sense in Soweto!'

You keep doors locked as you tool along these streets, and eyes wide open. In the space of 10 minutes, you pass a skirt fashioned from a Disney towel, 101 Dalmations cavorting across a robust rear; a red knitted hat folded flat and pinned jauntily to a budding Afro; and a leopard-print blanket 'shawl' teamed with fishnets and platform boots.

You also pass tethered goats and cattle, brought in for ritual ceremonies. Street barbers and more street walkers. Informal *spaza* shops with hand-painted signs that constitute a contemporary graphical lingo as lively as the *tsotsitaal* spoken here – a vivid mix of local languages, Afrikaans and slang. In Soweto, police stations sport uplifting slogans ('Moroka Police Station: together against crime'), and churches offer 'Weigh-less Meetings' and '24-seater [*sic*] couch for sale', along with salvation.

But it's the style in Soweto's homes that perhaps surprises most. Behind their exteriors of regimented township design, ingenuity and attention to detail create décor of distinctive character and overpowering charm. Think furnishing classics, clean-lined '50s kitchen chairs and cookers, worn enamel jugs and aluminium kettles, and walls and shelves vividly papered with magazine pages or packaging over-runs.

When even a modest Dralon sofa can be a major investment, suites are invariably cocooned in thick protective plastic, then made inviting with hand-crocheted arm covers and lovingly embroidered antimacassars. They proclaim everything from a family's soccer club allegiances ('Viva Pirates!') to its religious ones ('The Lord is my shepherd') and the hospitality that epitomises Soweto: 'Welcome visitors!'

Crowded as these homes may be, they're spacious compared to those in informal settlements, yet here too lie rich welcomes, offerings of beer, and an unmistakable style. Mavis Dlamini's *mkhukhu* in Diepkloof cost some R1 500 (US$150 or 150 Euros), measures barely three metres by three, and sleeps as many as six. 'My husband and I have the bed,' she explains, proudly parting tartan curtains that separate a mattress above painted storage boxes at one end of her meticulous tin house. 'The children sleep here on the floor,' and she indicates the sliver of polished lino between a miniscule fridge, a hotplate and a stand of shining pots, where her brood crouch on cushions watching Teletubbies on a portable TV.

The Tubbies' Noo-Noo robot is hoovering up a milk spill in their luxuriously roomy but sterile Lalaland den. 'I would like that thing better than a dog,' muses Mavis, 'but I think our house is nicer.'

There is no end to the enterprise of Soweto, and the style of homes to come stands already in the modest backyard of award-winning conservationist Mandla Mantoor on Soweto Mountain of Hope in Chiawelo. 'SoMoHo', as locals call it, is a windswept rise above the sprawl of settlements, where Mantoor holds gatherings for a slew of environmental and community development projects.

Mantoor's greatest hope is to empower Sowetans to support themselves from organic vegetable gardening, and house themselves in eco- and people-friendly structures. A simple *mkhukhu*-sized prototype is built of sandbags and recycled bottles, aesthetically appealing as it seems practical.

'It costs nothing, and stays warm in winter, cool in summer,' says SoMoHo Waste Creations project co-ordinator David Ngomane with passion. He was an activist in the '76 unrest and, since the new dispensation, has sought a way to contribute to the reconstruction of Soweto and his country. 'It is in work like this that we can find ourselves,' he concludes with conviction, adjusting the brim of a hat of woven carrier bags. 'We must just have faith. And we've always had faith in Soweto.'

life on the streets

On the streets of Soweto, speeding minibus taxis, vintage American sedans, German status models (a BMW here is dubbed a 'Be My Wife' or 'G-string'), and the occasional electric-green hearse career past patient donkeys pulling coal carts. On equally astonishing sidewalks, traders and buskers sell hubcaps and happiness, dagga (marijuana) and dances, skin creams and songs.

Vehicles here come with wings and attitude – polished, personalised, driven with pride.

Truckers rule in Soweto, transporting anything from goats to funeral-goers, and furniture to fences.

A Shangaan mealie seller gets her teeth into a sales pitch.

Business begins at home for Sowetans,

who feed basic local needs from their kitchen

windows, backyard shipping containers, converted

supermarket trolleys, or makeshift pavement tables.

Cabbages, cold beers or loose smokes, *my bra*?

Welcome to Soweto!

Stop by for a smoke any time ...

Traditional medicine markets are

everywhere in Soweto.

When mixed by a sangoma (traditional doctor

or herbalist), these roots, herbs and bark are

said to cure anything from the common cold

to cancer, while others serve as love potions.

This vast pavement pharmacy is directly opposite Chris Hani-Baragwanath Hospital,

one of South Africa's biggest training hospitals, and many Sowetans visit both.

The smile on the face of a child says everything about the exhilaration of growing up in Soweto. Even when they have little materially, most children here know they are cherished by their families and community. And life is an adventure, whether riding a bicycle (as this boy was doing), or playing soccer with empty cans on these throbbing streets.

Today, sponsored playgrounds and roadshows supplement the sparse and rusting (but still relished!) park equipment of old.

Young Soweto's favourite summer hangout is Orlando Swimming Pool, built largely

through the efforts of the late struggle activist, Archbishop Trevor Huddleston.

g games of Dice

countless street

ame is controlled

n, whose job it

dice, set up the

players if police

of these children,

approach.

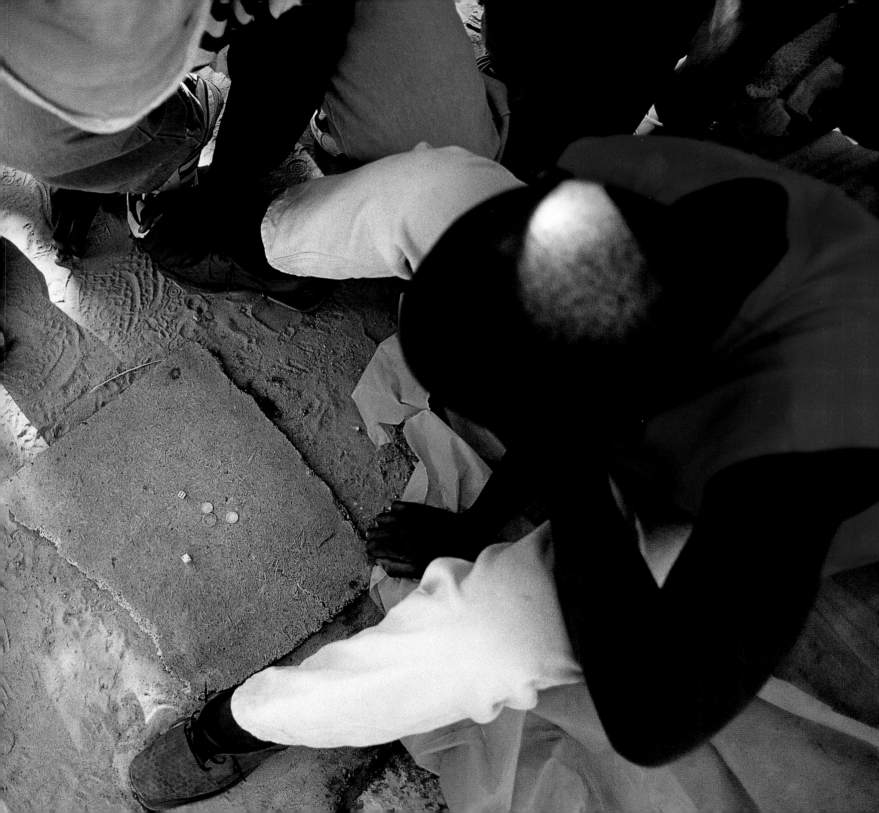

Come sundown, social life spills cheerfully from bite-sized backyards to the pavements, then drifts inevitably to the nearest shebeens. Here jazz flows and tellies flicker, while genial queens dispense advice for the heart, along with their home-brewed or commercial beer, once-banned 'white' liquor, and occasional cruder escape in **Kill Me Quick** or **Mbamba** – brown bread, yeast, hops and a head-blowing lot more.

cheers!

'Noise. It's the African way – we like it.'

At time of going to press, a quart of Castle cost just R5 (US$0.50, 0.50 Euros).

Tour operator Joe Motsogi (right) hangs out with a friend –
chilling, chatting, looking sharp.

LOUD AND PROUD

Shebeens broadcast as many brand names as spaza shops –
cost-effective décor, and cool.

Josephine Hlatswayo, proud co-owner of Soweto's DJ's Inn in Orlando East.

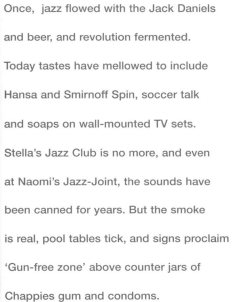

Once, jazz flowed with the Jack Daniels
and beer, and revolution fermented.
Today tastes have mellowed to include
Hansa and Smirnoff Spin, soccer talk
and soaps on wall-mounted TV sets.
Stella's Jazz Club is no more, and even
at Naomi's Jazz-Joint, the sounds have
been canned for years. But the smoke
is real, pool tables tick, and signs proclaim
'Gun-free zone' above counter jars of
Chappies gum and condoms.

Meet Wandie.

The rest of the world already has!

Most polished of Soweto's shebeens is Wandie's Place, favoured watering
hole of local business moguls and international tourists. They stop off by
the eager bus load to swig beer under brollies in the compact courtyard,
or to feast indoors on Western-friendly traditional fare under the reassuring
gaze of caged budgies and cockatiels, and to leave their cards on the walls.

The most toasted address in Soweto, and its most toasted hero.

Countless card-carrying diners can't be wrong.

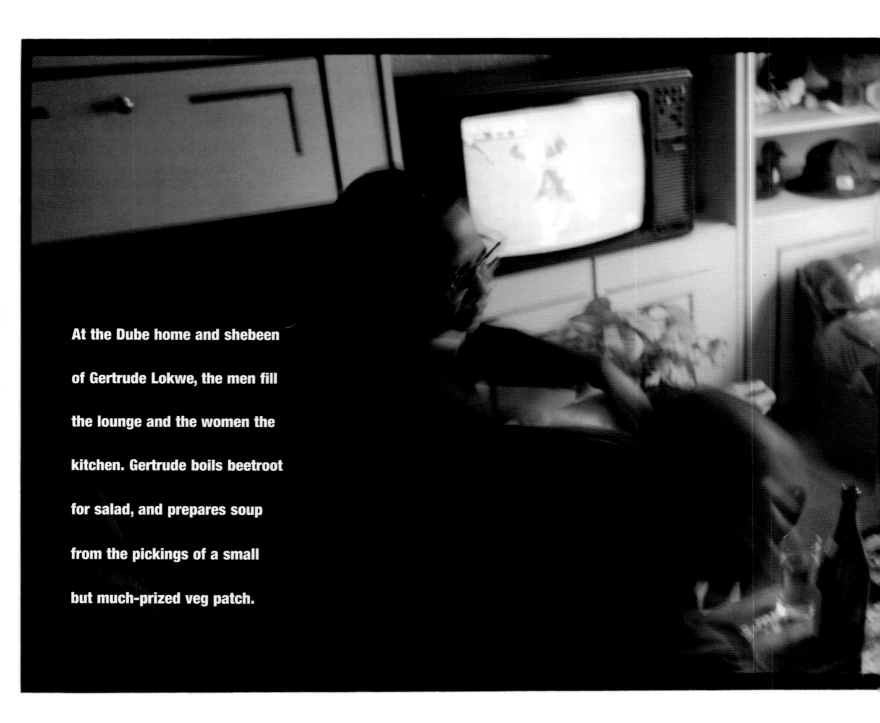

At the Dube home and shebeen

of Gertrude Lokwe, the men fill

the lounge and the women the

kitchen. Gertrude boils beetroot

for salad, and prepares soup

from the pickings of a small

but much-prized veg patch.

The passionate jazz of the past, the rousing syncopated guitars of *mbaqanga* and unifying militancy of freedom songs have given way to kick-ass *kwaito* and ubiquitous American musak. Soweto's jazzmen, in hot demand elsewhere, play less often at home, but still pour their souls into wedding celebrations and funerals. **Jazz will always have a place in the Soweto sun.**

signs of the times

We've got the numbers. Self-assigned street numbers give identity when you live in uniformity, and a semblance of stability when your home is a makeshift shack.

Red reflects the energy and warmth of the people.

If you have the will,
the wares and the
hand-written signs,
you're in business.

SPAZA SHOP, TUCK SHOP, FREE SHOP, STREET SHOP –
A SHOP BY ANY NAME WILL SELL AS SWEETLY.

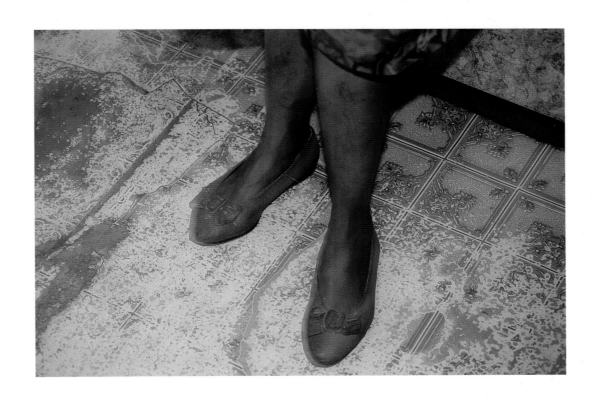

Diamonds on the soles of her shoes

Pattern plays everywhere in Soweto, from its corn-row houses to the funky

furnishings that line and enliven them, packaging over-runs to lino off-cuts.

Small buildings can carry big ambitions –

size of signage trumps size of structure every time.

In Soweto, the mural tradition begun on rural huts takes on the tastes of the city.

The People's Choice
Advertising is the street art of
Soweto – hand-painted billboards
become arresting murals.

Hanging out at street shops, you can watch your world walk by.

Shops sing out their brand allegiances with pride – choruses of consumerism
constantly repeated in changing keys.

A container butchery gives new meaning to the term 'canned' meat.

DEALS ON WHEELS
Mobile dry-cleaners are synonymous with Soweto.

Mageu is a drink made from fermented maize porridge, sometimes flavoured with bananas and other fruits.

MAGEU

R1-50 Per Litre

SPECIAL BREW

AWETHU

R1-50 Per Litre

Sowetans are past masters at the proclamation of personal style. When other forms of freedom were curtailed, a man could still shrug on his Sunday suit and be a man. A woman could slip from a maid's uniform into a lay-by two-piece and

SMASHING FASHION

well-polished heels, shake free her braids, and be a woman. Far from restricting fashion choice, poverty has propelled it towards careful quality selection, and a sure, often ingenious, individual touch. **Très chic.**

Sowetans take out their traditional best for weddings,
and for South Africa's Heritage Day each September 24.

Formal suits

or soft sarongs,

cowboy plaids or

seshweshwe (German prints),

fly shades or *doeks* (scarves)

wrapped like butterfly wings …

Attitude is all.

STREET SMART

Urban cowboys score,

but trainers and track tops rule

for playing it cool.

Beyond the broken fences and uniformity

that overshadow even bold attempts at individualising exteriors

with faux slasto and painted railings,

lie homes of warmth and defiant creativity.

home talk

THE NELSON MANDELA SQUATTER CAMP

Eager to settle near Johannesburg, city of golden employment dreams, informal settlers carve hard lives in homes of cardboard and old iron on any scrap of land. Soweto's Nelson Mandela Camp was one of the most famous, a shock of shacks where children and chickens played in the dirt, but people kept spirit and pride. Bulldozers demolished the camp in 2002. Its people dispersed, only images now remain.

1990 – 2002

THE NELSON MANDELA SQUATTER CAMP 1990 – 2002

The great re-cycle of life

No sooner had the Nelson Mandela Squatter Camp been
demolished, than its rubble was retrieved to rise again elsewhere.

For all their wrenching poverty,

there are elements of undeniable

visual beauty in informal settlements,

born of the jigsaw juxtaposition

of salvaged metal and wood,

and rich splashes of colour.

Soweto boasts a number of millionaires (some 23 at time of going to print), but most retreat to leafy Johannesburg suburbia. Those who remain favour face-brick edifices wrapped impassively in massive walls studded with security cameras.

fences

basic homes

like these in Soweto's Orlando sector
and White City, are evolving with their
owners into a growing middle class –
an inventive extension here, a tiled roof
or a wrought-iron gate there. It's a style
blend that is strangely but inescapably
chic, before toppling into the
blandness of big-money mansions.

Sowetans love to garden, giving the most modest home a certain charm.

People here show proud faces to the world, with ornamental walls and railings, and well-swept sidewalks.

Kitchens are the warm centres of Soweto's crowded homes, where children help women cook big meals the traditional way. Presiding in most, despite electrification, are sturdy coal stoves – dignified presences amid the impertinent appurtenances of modern convenience living, from flashy Formica counters to bright plastic plates.

KITCHEN CHIC

The past sits comfortably here

Retro chic rules when finances bite, and furnishings and appliances
go second-hand – simple classics chosen for quality and durability,
and carefully tended and shone.

Search

and you'll discover an Aladdin's cave
of functional beauty in Sowetan homes.

Traditional cooking spoons

Moses Radebe and his family, like thousands of Sowetans,
sit down to a Sunday lunch of *pap*, chicken and veg.

Look back with pride

Sense of family is strong in Soweto and portraits are prominently displayed, often in eclectic mixes with furniture-shop prints, traditional masks and tapestry hangings.

The past opens onto the present

God is everywhere

'Christ gave His hands for you,' a guide gravely informs visitors below this broken statue in Regina Mundi Catholic Church in Moroka. 'When you stop using them, you must give them back.'

Into the arms of Christ … Regina Mundi provided refuge during unrest, a place to mourn the struggle dead, and a seat for the Truth and Reconciliation Commission.

A few churches have become too dilapidated to use (opposite), but Sowetans keep carrying the faith elsewhere. This couple is marrying in the Lutheran Church, Meadowlands.

The Shembe Church, founded by the late Zulu prophet Isaiah Shembe in 1911, is the oldest African Independant Church in southern Africa, and along with the Zionist Christian Church, one of the largest, with an enthusiastic Sowetan following. Shembe scriptures blend traditional Zulu beliefs, Old Testament references and reworked turn-of-the-century European and American Protestant missionary gospel traditions.

Sweep of faith

Soweto has a small but growing Muslim community centred on Dlamini Mosque. Township youths began turning to Islam in the turbulent '70s, attracted by the Qur'anic teachings of universal brotherhood. Numbers have swollen from fewer than 12 in 1976 to some 2 000 worshippers at the mosque today.

Soweto food

Gertrude Lokwe's Spicy Lentil Soup

Isobho

GERTRUDE LOKWE'S SPICY LENTIL SOUP

When we arrived at Gertrude Lokwe's tiny shebeen on a fresh winter's morning, she was preparing this hearty lentil soup. The secret weapon in her compact kitchen was her grater, which she used for almost all the ingredients. This soup is best served with some steamed bread.

1 large onion, grated
2 cloves garlic, crushed
1 Tbsp sunflower oil
1 Tbsp masala (curry powder)
2 cups brown lentils or split peas
3 large carrots, grated
4 tomatoes, diced
2 large potatoes, peeled and grated
4 cups water
salt and white pepper to taste

Fry the onion and garlic in the oil until translucent. Add the curry powder and fry for a minute, stirring. Add the rest of the ingredients and simmer over medium heat for 20 minutes, stirring constantly. Reduce heat to low and simmer for a further 10 minutes until the lentils are soft. Season and serve hot. If preferred, add a dollop of sour cream and some chopped parsley to finish it off. Serves 4.

Mealies (maize or corn) were introduced to Africa in the late 16th century. Because mealies are so similiar to the traditional African grain sorghum, and are easy to cultivate and grow rapidly, they quickly became a basic crop in many parts of the continent. In South Africa, mealies are the staple food. Eaten whole, hot off the braai (barbecue), or ground into mealie meal and cooked as porridge (*pap*) to be eaten as a thick, savoury accompaniment to a main meal or with milk and sugar for breakfast, mealies provide a cheap, tax-free source of energy for a growing nation.

Roasted mealies

In mealie season (from around November to February), vendors on the outskirts of Soweto and in Johannesburg's city centre tend brazier-fires and sell braaied mealies to commuters and passers-by. While still in its husk, the mealie is simply placed on a grid over hot coals and turned every few minutes. Once cooked, it can be seasoned with salt and pepper or basted with butter or margarine.

Pap is a stiff, steamed porridge usually made from mealie meal, and is a staple of 90 per cent of Africa's population. It's filling and sustaining, especially combined with vitamin-rich *morogo* (a variety of spinach). *Pap* can be served hot or, after it has cooled, it can be fried, giving it a different texture. Sowetans especially enjoy it with chakalaka, a type of relish. *Pap* has become a popular side-dish at the braais of all South Africans.

2 cups mealie meal
1 tsp margarine
2 cups boiling water
salt to taste

Add mealie meal and margarine to salted boiling water. Cover saucepan and cook over low heat for 5 minutes. Remove lid and stir occasionally until well cooked. Test by throwing a small ball of *pap* against the wall. If it is done, it will bounce off the wall. If it sticks, it needs to cook longer. Serves 4.

To make *isigwagane*, cook the *pap* as described above, then mix in 2 cups of cooked sugar beans. The texture should be dry and crumbly so that you can eat it with your fingers. Serve with chakalaka (page 150) and a cup of hot, sweet tea.

Pap with Chakalaka

Sowetan meals are more about the sharing than the eating

SAMP AND BEANS

2 cups samp
2 cups beans (sugar beans, kidney beans)
salt and freshly ground black pepper to taste
2 medium potatoes, peeled and cubed
marrow bones (optional)

Wash the samp and beans well. Place in a saucepan, cover with cold water, bring to the boil and simmer over medium heat
for at least 4 hours. Add seasoning. Add the potatoes and, if using, add marrow bones for extra flavour.
While cooking, always add cold water when additional liquid is needed. This dish can be served on its own,
but is also excellent with lamb or chicken. Serves 8.

130

Umngqusho

SAMP AND BEANS WITH ONION

This traditional dish is simmered for a long time until everything is tender.

1 kg samp and bean mix, rinsed and soaked overnight
salt to taste

ONION MIXTURE
2 onions, sliced
2 cloves garlic, crushed (optional)
2 green chillies, chopped
sunflower oil
½ tsp whole cloves
1 tsp allspice
½ tsp grated nutmeg
freshly ground black pepper
10 tsp butter (optional)

Pour off the water after soaking and place the samp and bean mix in a large saucepan. Cover with water and simmer slowly until the samp and beans are nearly soft and most of the water has evaporated. (Add more cold water if necessary.) Season well with salt.
In the meantime, sauté the onions, garlic and chillies in a little oil until soft. Add the cloves and allspice. Add the onion mixture to the samp and continue to simmer until the samp mixture is completely soft. Season with nutmeg and black pepper. Add extra salt to taste, if necessary. Stir in the butter if using. Serve hot with meat and gravy if desired. Serves 10–12.

Simple, tasty, and able to feed many mouths – you don't need any other reasons for explaining the popularity of these dishes. Malay slaves and indentured Indian workers brought South Africa the curries of their homelands, and a multitude of colourful spices. Bredies are synonymous with Cape Malay cuisine, but Sowetans too relish these appetizing, spicy stews of meat and vegetables.

Stews, Curries and Bredies

TOMATO BREDIE

5 tsp butter (or margarine, lard or sunflower oil)
2 large onions, sliced
1 clove garlic, crushed
1.5 kg stewing lamb or mutton, cubed
2 tsp salt
freshly ground black pepper
a little stock, water or wine
500 g potatoes, sliced
1 kg medium tomatoes, skinned and chopped
1 tsp white sugar
½ tsp dried thyme
1 tsp chopped fresh marjoram

Heat the butter in a large saucepan and sauté the onions and garlic for about 5 minutes or until the onions are translucent. Add the meat and brown quickly on all sides. Add the salt, pepper and stock, water or wine and simmer, covered, for 1½–2 hours, or until the meat starts to soften. Add the remaining ingredients and simmer for a further hour. Serve with *pap*, rice or samp. Serves 4.

Spicy Mutton Masala Curry

A potjie is a three-legged cast-iron pot that is traditionally placed over coals. The secret to a good potjie is patience. Layer the ingredients and do not be tempted to mix them all up. You can reproduce this recipe just as effectively using a thick-bottomed pot on a stove.

3 Tbsp sunflower oil
salt and freshly ground black pepper to taste
2 kg mutton chops
2 large onions, coarsely chopped
3 bay leaves
3 large potatoes, peeled and cubed
1 cup uncooked rice
1 cup dried apricots, soaked in water for 1 hour and drained
1 cup water
½ cup frozen mealies
½ cup frozen peas
1 cup chutney
4 tsp strong curry powder
1 tsp turmeric
½ tsp ground coriander
½ tsp grated nutmeg

Heat the oil in the pot. Season the meat and brown a few pieces at a time in the pot. Remove the meat and set aside. Fry the onions until tender. Return the meat to the pot with the onions and bay leaves. Arrange the potatoes, rice and apricots in layers on top of the meat. Add the water. Cover and simmer for 1 hour. Add more water if the potjie boils dry. Add the mealies and peas.

Mix the remaining ingredients together, then add the mixture to the potjie. Cover and simmer for 30–45 minutes. Serve with sliced banana, finely chopped onion and tomato and finely grated coconut. Serves 8.

Green Bean Bredie

Bredies are cooked without adding extra water so that the juices of the meat add the flavour to the dish. This style of cooking was common among most of the shebeen queens interviewed. They have a preference for using pre-prepared spices (such as Robertsons Chicken Spice), but this recipe uses ginger, thyme and chilli.

2 Tbsp oil
500 g stewing lamb
1 cup coarsely chopped onion
3 cloves garlic, minced
1 tsp minced fresh root ginger
½ cup water
2 cups fresh green beans, trimmed and cut into 3 cm-lengths
2 medium potatoes, peeled and cubed
1 green chilli, chopped
a pinch of dried thyme
salt and freshly ground black pepper to taste

Heat the oil in a large saucepan over moderate heat. Add the lamb and brown it in batches. Remove and set aside. Add the onions, garlic and ginger to the saucepan and cook over low heat until translucent. Return the meat to the saucepan. Cover tightly, and simmer for 30 minutes over the lowest heat. Add the remaining ingredients and bring to the boil. Cover again, reduce heat, and simmer for about 1 hour, stirring occasionally. If you prefer your green beans less cooked, add them 5 minutes before serving to that they retain their crispness. Taste for seasoning and serve immediately with dumplings. Serves 4.

Chicken Livers with Mealie Meal

Chicken Livers with Mealie Meal

1 tub (250 g) fresh chicken livers
salt and freshly ground black pepper to taste
1 cup mealie meal
2 Tbsp sunflower oil

Remove any gristle from the chicken livers and season. Pour the mealie meal onto a plate and roll each liver in the meal, coating thoroughly. Heat the oil in a frying pan and fry off the livers for about 5 minutes until cooked through. Serve with *pap* and chopped tomato and chakalaka (page 150). Serves 4.

Curried Beans

This is a simple recipe for a saucy bean dish,
and is ideal served with pap.

1 Tbsp masala (curry powder)
1 Tbsp sunflower oil
410 g can red kidney beans
410 g can baked beans in tomato sauce
410 g can butter beans
⅖ cup water

Fry the curry powder in oil over a low heat to release the flavour. Add all the beans and stir. Add water, heat through and serve warm or chilled as a salad. Serves 6.

Curried Beans with *Pap*

2 Tbsp vegetable oil
3 cups chopped cabbage
1 onion, chopped
5 carrots, grated
1 green chilli, seeded and chopped
salt and freshly ground black pepper

Stir-fry all the ingredients

in a large pan over high heat,

then cover with a lid to steam

for the last 5–10 minutes.

Check seasoning and serve

as a side dish. Serves 4.

Soweto Fried Cabbage

vetkoek

FAT CAKES

1 cup cake flour
½ tsp salt
1 tsp baking powder
1 egg
milk
sunflower oil for deep-frying

Sift the dry ingredients into a bowl. Beat the egg
lightly in a cup and add to the dry ingredients. Add
sufficient milk to make a smooth, thick batter. Heat
the oil in a pan and carefully drop large spoonfuls of
the batter into the hot oil. Fry, turning them over
now and then, until golden brown. Cut open, butter,
and fill. Makes 8–10 small vetkoek.

Made from a simple milk, egg and flour batter,

these deep-fried dough balls are a filling snack, probably first eaten by the pioneering

Voortrekkers in their ox-wagons. Delicious smeared with butter and jam (jelly)

or stuffed with savoury mince.

Morogo and Spinach

*Green leaves are a favourite in the Sowetan kitchen and wild spinach (morogo) takes
pride of place. Alternatives are the new green shoots of pumpkins and squashes,
the unblemished flavoursome leaves of beetroot or the widely available Swiss chard (spinach).*

Pick only the freshest new shoots, peel the skins off the stems if necessary and wash thoroughly. Chop very finely.

Pumpkin Shoots and Potato

1 large onion, chopped
1 Tbsp sunflower oil
6 cups finely chopped new pumpkin shoots
1 cup water
2 large potatoes, peeled and chopped
1 green chilli, chopped (optional)
salt and white pepper to taste

Fry the onion in the oil, add the pumpkin shoots and fry over a low heat until wilted.
Add the water and the potatoes and cook until the potatoes are soft. Add the chilli if you like *voomah*!
Season and serve with *pap*. Serves 4.

Dried morogo,
ready to be reconstituted with water

Swiss Chard and Onion with Roasted Peanuts

2 bunches Swiss chard (spinach)
1 cup water
1 large onion, chopped
50 g peanuts
½ tsp salt

Wash the Swiss chard in cold water. Remove the stalks and discard. Chop the leaves. Bring the water to the boil in a saucepan, and add the chopped leaves and onion. Cook until the leaves have wilted. Meanwhile, roast the peanuts in a frying pan, then add the salt to the peanuts in the pan. Crush the peanuts, add them to the cooked spinach and simmer until the flavours have infused.

Serve as a side dish with *pap* and meat. Serves 4.

Pan-fried Sweet Potatoes

Pan-fried Sweet Potatoes

675–900 g sweet potatoes
juice of 1 lemon
salt
1 Tbsp cake flour
a good pinch of cayenne pepper
about 3 Tbsp sunflower oil
1 large onion, chopped
115 g streaky bacon, chopped
¾ cup fresh brown or white breadcrumbs

Peel the sweet potatoes and cut into 4-cm cubes. Place in a saucepan of boiling water with the lemon juice and a little salt and simmer for 8–10 minutes until cooked but still firm.

Mix together the flour, cayenne pepper and a pinch of salt. Drain the potatoes and then dust with the seasoned flour, making sure the pieces are well coated.

Heat 1 Tbsp of the oil in a large frying pan and fry the onion for about 2 minutes. Add the bacon and fry over a gentle heat for 6–8 minutes until the onion and bacon are golden. Transfer to a plate using a slotted spoon. Add the breadcrumbs to the pan and fry, stirring, for about 1–2 minutes until golden. Add to the plate containing the bacon and onion.

Heat the remaining oil in the pan and fry the potatoes for 5–6 minutes, turning occasionally, until evenly browned. Add the breadcrumb and bacon mixture and cook for 1 minute. Serve as a side dish with *pap* and meat. Serves 4.

Raw Sweet-and-Sour Beetroot Salad

Boiled beetroot salad pickled with loads of vinegar is very common, but this raw version is rather interesting.

4 large raw beetroots, peeled and grated
¾ cup vinegar
3 Tbsp white sugar
4 tsp salt

Heat the vinegar, sugar and salt over a low heat until the sugar has dissolved. Pour the warm mixture over the grated beetroot and mix thoroughly. Serve chilled as a side dish with *pap* and meat. Serves 4.

Everybody has their own version of this glorious and unique South African taste

sensation. Three of South Africa's major food producers now make their own versions

in varying degrees of chilli heat which are available at supermarkets.

Chakalaka

2 Tbsp sunflower oil
1 onion, finely chopped
1 clove garlic, crushed
1 green pepper, chopped
½ cabbage, shredded
½ cauliflower, broken into small florets
3 carrots, grated or julienned
2–3 chillies (depending on taste)
2 tomatoes, chopped
410 g can baked beans in tomato sauce (optional)
salt to taste

Heat the oil and fry the onion, garlic and pepper until soft. Add cabbage, cauliflower
and carrots and cook until limp. Add remaining ingredients and simmer for about 10 minutes.
Serve as a side dish at braais or over *pap*. Serves 8–10.

Chakalaka

This is one of the most common chakalakas *at buy-and-braai establishments.*
The secret is to chop the ingredients as finely as possible, so be patient.

4 red or green chillies
3 ripe tomatoes
1 onion
a handful of fresh coriander leaves
salt and freshly ground black pepper to taste

Chop the chillies, tomatoes and onion.

Mix in coriander and season. Leave to settle.

Serves 8 as a side dish with a dollop of *pap*.

Fresh Onion, Tomato and Coriander *Chakalaka*

The words Pili-Pili, Piri-Piri and Peri-Peri are all used to refer to hot chile (chilli) peppers and the sauce and marinades made from them, as well as to foods cooked with those sauces and marinades. This spicy, hot rub can be used on chicken, beef, fish or seafood before grilling.

Peri-Peri Rub

2–3 fresh hot chilli peppers (red peppers are typical), chopped
¼ cup lemon juice, lime juice or cider vinegar
¼ cup sunflower oil
1 Tbsp cayenne pepper or dried red pepper flakes
1 Tbsp paprika
1 tsp salt
1 tsp minced garlic or garlic powder

Combine all the ingredients and grind and mix to a smooth paste. Adjust the ratio of cayenne pepper to paprika to taste. Rub the mixture onto meat or fish and allow to marinate in a glass bowl for at least 30 minutes before cooking.

Peri-Peri

Achaar (also known as atchaar or atchar)
is a relish introduced to South Africa
about a century ago.

Achaar

Mango Achaar

1.5 kg green mangoes, peeled, stoned and cut into 2-cm chunks
2 cups white vinegar
250 g white sugar
2 onions, sliced
¼ cup chopped root ginger
1 tsp cayenne pepper
1 tsp mustard seeds
2 cloves garlic, crushed
5 whole peppercorns
1 tsp salt

Boil all the ingredients until the mango chunks are tender, but still
whole. Pour into hot, sterilized jars and seal.

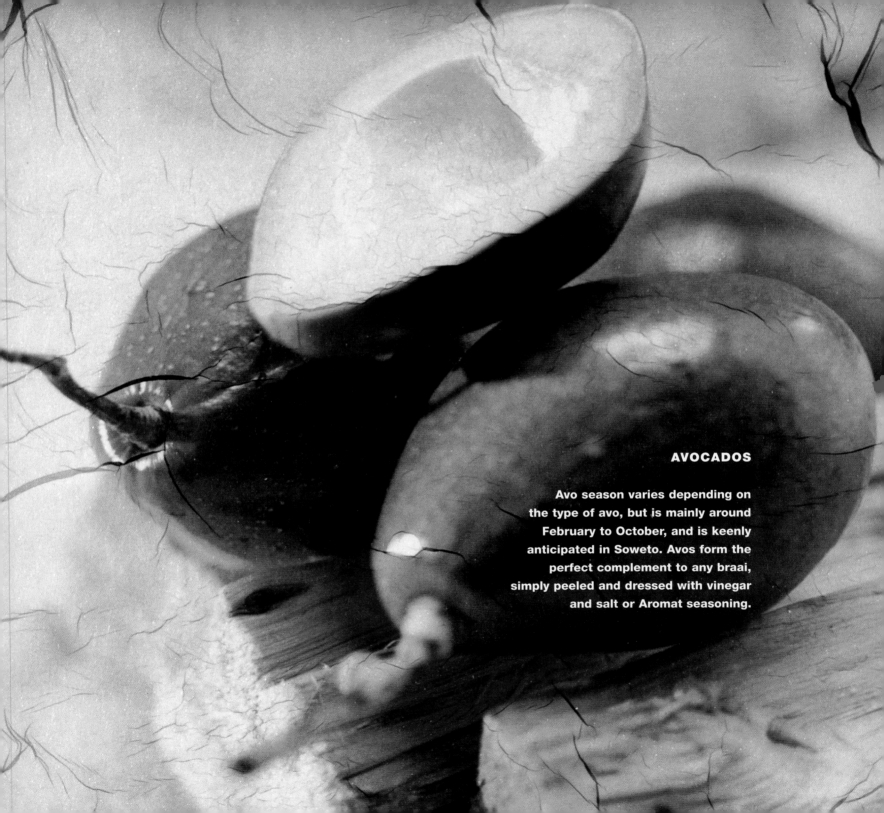

AVOCADOS

Avo season varies depending on the type of avo, but is mainly around February to October, and is keenly anticipated in Soweto. Avos form the perfect complement to any braai, simply peeled and dressed with vinegar and salt or Aromat seasoning.

Although we didn't come across anybody actually making ginger beer in their homes, the brand Stoney is huge in the townships. And quite rightly so. Nothing on earth refreshes like ginger beer.

Cheers!

Home-made Ginger Beer

4.5 litres water
30 g root ginger, crushed
2 cups white sugar
1 Tbsp active dry yeast

Bring the water to the boil, then add the ginger and sugar. Remove from the stove and cool until lukewarm. Add the yeast and leave, covered, for 1–2 days. Strain the beer into sterilized bottles and seal. Refrigerate and serve chilled. The ginger beer will keep in the fridge for a week.

King Korn is a popular home brew dry mix.
It is added to water and mealie meal
porridge and allowed to ferment for three days.
A favourite at traditional ceremonies, weddings
and other special occasions.

traditional taste

Before commercial beer was introduced, sorghum beer was the

traditional drink of the townships, and sorghum shebeens still exist today.

Drink to that!

National Sorghum Breweries

iJUBA

SPECIAL

OBUNGCONO

OKWEMPILO NAMANDLA

QUALITY TESTED

1 litre

SPECIAL BEER

WE KEEP ENVIRONMENT CLEAN